CAMBRIDGE LIBRARY COLLECTION

Books of enduring scholarly value

Music

The systematic academic study of music gave rise to works of description, analysis and criticism, by composers and performers, philosophers and anthropologists, historians and teachers, and by a new kind of scholar - the musicologist. This series makes available a range of significant works encompassing all aspects of the developing discipline.

Anecdotes of George Frederick Handel, and John Christopher Smith

The author and clergyman William Coxe (1748–1828), noted for his travel works, was the stepson of Handel's amanuensis, German-born John Christopher Smith (1712–1795). First published in 1799, the present work is a valuable source of first-hand information about two men at the heart of eighteenth-century English music: George Frideric Handel (1685–1759), whose inventive and sensitive melodic genius and exuberant brilliance in depicting the spectacular are best displayed in his *Messiah* and *Zadok the Priest*, and Smith, a composer of attractive and fashionable music, who settled in London in 1720, took lessons with Handel and later supported the great composer as his eyesight failed. Smith was also organist at the Foundling Hospital until 1770. This publication, profits from which were intended to support Smith's family, draws on the works of John Hawkins and Charles Burney, and on anecdotes claimed to be 'derived from unquestionable authority'.

Cambridge University Press has long been a pioneer in the reissuing of out-of-print titles from its own backlist, producing digital reprints of books that are still sought after by scholars and students but could not be reprinted economically using traditional technology. The Cambridge Library Collection extends this activity to a wider range of books which are still of importance to researchers and professionals, either for the source material they contain, or as landmarks in the history of their academic discipline.

Drawing from the world-renowned collections in the Cambridge University Library and other partner libraries, and guided by the advice of experts in each subject area, Cambridge University Press is using state-of-the-art scanning machines in its own Printing House to capture the content of each book selected for inclusion. The files are processed to give a consistently clear, crisp image, and the books finished to the high quality standard for which the Press is recognised around the world. The latest print-on-demand technology ensures that the books will remain available indefinitely, and that orders for single or multiple copies can quickly be supplied.

The Cambridge Library Collection brings back to life books of enduring scholarly value (including out-of-copyright works originally issued by other publishers) across a wide range of disciplines in the humanities and social sciences and in science and technology.

Anecdotes of
George Frederick
Handel
and John Christopher Smith

With Select Pieces of Music,
Composed by J.C. Smith,
Never Before Published

WILLIAM COXE

CAMBRIDGE
UNIVERSITY PRESS

University Printing House, Cambridge, CB2 8BS, United Kingdom

Published in the United States of America by Cambridge University Press, New York

Cambridge University Press is part of the University of Cambridge.
It furthers the University's mission by disseminating knowledge in the pursuit of
education, learning and research at the highest international levels of excellence.

www.cambridge.org
Information on this title: www.cambridge.org/9781108070942

© in this compilation Cambridge University Press 2014

This edition first published 1799
This digitally printed version 2014

ISBN 978-1-108-07094-2 Paperback

ANECDOTES

OF

GEORGE FREDERICK HANDEL,

AND

JOHN CHRISTOPHER SMITH.

E. Harding sc.t

GEORGE FREDERICK HANDEL,

From an Original Picture Painted by Denner

Publiſhed May 1.1799,by Cadell & Davies,Strand.

ANECDOTES

OF

GEORGE FREDERICK HANDEL,

AND

JOHN CHRISTOPHER SMITH.

———

WITH

SELECT PIECES OF MUSIC,

COMPOSED

BY J. C. SMITH,

NEVER BEFORE PUBLISHED.

———

LONDON:

PRINTED BY W. BULMER AND CO.
SOLD BY CADELL AND DAVIES, STRAND; E. HARDING, PALL-MALL;
BIRCHALL, MUSIC-SELLER, BOND-STREET; AND
J. EATON, SALISBURY.
1799.

TO

MR. PETER COXE,

IN GRATITUDE,

AS WELL FOR VARIOUS

COMMUNICATIONS AND JUDICIOUS REMARKS,

AS FOR HIS STRENUOUS EXERTIONS

IN PROMOTING THE SUBSCRIPTION,

AND AS

A MEMORIAL OF PRIVATE FRIENDSHIP,

THESE ANECDOTES

ARE INSCRIBED.

Bemerton,
April 20, 1799.

ADVERTISEMENT.

In submitting to the Public, Anecdotes of Handel, some apology may be expected, as his Life has been already given in numerous productions. The motives which gave rise to this attempt, must plead an excuse. The profits of this Publication being appropriated to the use of the Relations of Mr. Smith, whose Memoirs are now first presented to the world.

For the Memoirs of Handel, the best printed accounts have been consulted. " The Memoirs of the Life of George Frederick Handel, 8vo. 1760," which were written under the inspection of Mr. Smith;" " Sir John Hawkins's History of Music:"—" an Account of the Musical Performances in Commemoration of Handel;" " the present State of Music in Germany and the Netherlands;" and, " the History of Music;" all by Dr. Burney. Some original Anecdotes are interspersed, derived from unquestionable authority.

The Portrait of Handel is engraven from an original picture painted by Denner, in 1736 or 1737, which Handel gave to Mr. Smith; who left it to his son-in-law, the Rev. William Coxe, in whose possession it now remains. The Portrait of Mr. Smith is engraven from a picture by Zoffani, now in the possession of Mr. Peter Coxe.

LIST OF SUBSCRIBERS.

The Names of the Subscribers for fine Paper Copies are marked with*.

Adolphus, Mr.
Anderson, John, Esq.
* Angerstein, John Julius, Esq.
Astle, Thomas, Esq. Keeper of the Re-
   cords, Tower

Bagwill, John, Esq.
* Balfour, Blaney, Esq.
Balfour, Mrs.
Balfour, Miss
Barnes, Rev. F. Master of Peter House,
   Cambridge
* Barnes, John, Esq.
* Baronneau, Francis, Esq.
* Barrington, Hon. Daines, 5 Copies
* Barrington, Hon. Admiral
* Bath and Wells, the Lord Bishop of
Beatniffe, Mr.
* Beckingham, Rev. John Charles
Bell, William, Esq.
Bentham, Miss, Oxford.
Birchall, Mr. Music-seller, Bond-street,
   18 Copies
Bird, William, Esq.
* Blaney, Rev. Dr. Christ's Ch. Oxford
Bowdon, William, Esq.
* Braybrook, Lord, 5 Copies
Bremner, Mr. Bookseller, 3 Copies.
Brogham, Rev. John
* Brooksbank, Mrs. 5 Copies
Brooke, Rev. Richard
* Bryant, Jacob, Esq.
* Bryan, Michael, Esq.
Bull, Robert, Esq.

Bureau, James, Esq.
Burrell, Mr. Charles
Burrows, Capt. Thomas

* Cadell and Davies, Messrs. 10 Copies
* Call, Lady
* Call, Miss
Callender, Henry, Esq.
* Cancellor, John, Esq.
Carr, Rev. Mr.
* Chalmers, George, Esq.
Chalmers, Charles, Esq.
* Chaloner, George, Esq.
Champion, Alexander, Esq.
Champion, Benjamin, Esq.
Chard, Mr. Winchester
Christie, Robert, Esq.
Clinton, Hon. Mrs.
Cock, Mr.
Cole, Benjamin, Esq.
Colkett, ———, Esq.
Collier, J. P. Esq.
Combe, Boyce, Esq.
Cotton, Mrs. S. Bath
* Coxe, Rev. William, 5 Copies
* Coxe, Edward, Esq. 5 Copies
* Coxe, Peter, Esq. 5 Copies
* Coxe, Rev. George, 5 Copies
* Coxe, Mrs. Emilia, 5 Copies
Crokatt, Henry, Esq.
Crotch, Mr. Oxford
Crowl, C. Esq.
Cure, Capel, Esq.
* Curtis, Rev. J. A. Vicar of Bitton

b

* Dampier, Rev. Dr. Dean of Rochester
  Dance, Rev. Thomas, Downton
* D'Aranda, Mrs. Putney
  Davison, Craufurd, Esq.
  Dean, John, Esq.
* De la Cour, William, Esq.
  Delap, Samuel, Esq.
  Delap, Mrs.
  Delap, Miss Mary Ann
  Dinsley, Mr. William
  Du Bois, C. H. Esq.
* Durham, the Hon. and Right Rev. the
  Lord Bishop of, 2 Copies

  Easton, Mr. Bookseller, Salisbury, 14
  Copies
* Egremont, the Earl of, 5 Copies
  Erwin, Edward, Esq.
* Eyre, the Rev. Dr. Canon of Sarum.

* Faulder, Mr. Bookseller, 7 Copies
* Fawkner, William, Esq.
  Field, Mr. Organist, Bath.
  Fisher, Rev. Dr. Canon of Windsor
* Fitzwilliam, Lord Viscount, 4 Copies
  Forster, Rev. Dr. Canon of Windsor
  Forster, Rev. Dr. Norwich
  Forsyth, James, Esq.
  Foster, Mr. Charles
  Fraser, William, Esq.
* Freeling, Francis, Esq. Secretary to the
  Post Masters General

* Gardner, Mr. William, 2 Copies
  Gawen, Miss Eliza
* Gillbee, William, Esq.
  Gillon, John, Esq.
* Goldsworthy, Lieutenant General, 2
  Copies
  Golightly, William, Esq.
* Gregg, Thomas, Esq.
* Grey de Wilton, Lord

* Harding, Mr. E. No. 98, Pall-Mall,
  19 Copies
* Hardwicke, Earl of, 2 Copies
  Harrington, Dr.
  Harris, Miss Louisa
  Hartley, Mrs. M. Bath,
  Henslow, Mrs. Chatham Yard
  Hetley, Rev. H. Wilton
  Hibbut, Mr. Fellow of King's College,
  Cambridge
  Hippuff, Charles, Esq.
* Hoare, Sir R. C. Bart. 2 Copies
* Holroyd, Mrs. Bath, 5 Copies
  Horden, Mr. Peterborough
* Humphreys, Mrs. Bath

* Ingles, Rev. Henry
  Irving, John, Esq.
  Jacob, Rev. Mr. Salisbury
  Jennings, John, Esq.

* Keene, Benjamin, Esq.
  King's Library
  King's College Library
  Kirwan, Anthony, Esq.

* Law, Edward, Esq.
* Le Blanc, Simon, Esq. 5 Copies
  Leckie, George, Esq.
* Leeds, Duke of, 2 Copies
* Leigh, John, Esq. Bath
* Leycester, Hugh, Esq. 5 Copies
  Lyon, George, Esq.

  Maddison, John, Esq.
  Mainwaring, Rev. Mr.
* Malmesbury, Lord, 2 Copies
* Maltby, Miss
  Maule, Rev. Mr.
  Melmoth, Mrs.
  Meyer, John, Esq. Clapham, 3 Copies
  Meyer, John, Esq. M. D.
  Middleton, Rev. T. F.

M'Intosh, John, Esq.
Mitchell, William, Esq.
Montgomery, Miss
Montgomery, Miss Mary
Morton, Charles, Esq.
* Moss, Rev. C. D. D. Canon Residentiary of St. Paul's
Musgrave, Sir William, Bart.

* Napier, Lady
* Nesbitt, John, Esq. M. P.
Newcastle, Duchess of
* Newton, Francis, Esq.
Nichols, Mr. Printer, 2 Copies
Nicol, Mr. Bookseller, Pall-Mall
Nugent, Miss
Nugent, Miss Henrietta

Ogden, Mrs. Salisbury
Ogle, William Meade, Esq.
Ord, Mrs.

* Pack, Miss, Prestwould, near Loughborough, Leicestershire, 5 Copies
Parry, Thomas, Esq.
Parsons, Miss, Oxford
* Payne, Mr. Bookseller, 8 Copies
* Peachy, Hon. John
* Pembroke, Countess of, 5 Copies
* Pembroke, the Earl of, 5 Copies
* Pennant, Thomas, Esq.
Pettiward, Roger, Esq.
Philpott, Mr. Bath
Pim, William, Esq.
* Pillans, W. C. Esq.
* Platt, John, Esq.
* Porter, William, Esq.
Potts, James, Esq.
* Pretyman, Rev. Dr. Prebendary of Norwich.
* Price, Uvedale, Esq. 5 Copies
* Price, Rev. Robert, D. D. Prebendary of Durham, 5 Copies
* Price, William, Esq. 5 Copies
Puget, Mrs.

* Pusey, Hon. Philip, 10 Copies

* Quin, Mrs. Bath

Ravenhill, John, Esq.
Rivaz, V. F. Esq.
* Rivers, Lady, Winchester, 5 Copies
* Rivers, Sir Thomas, Bart. 5 Copies
* Rivers, James, Esq.
* Rivers, Miss
* Roberts, Thomas, Esq.
Robinson, Hon. Mrs.
* Robson, Mr. Bookseller, 2 Copies
Rogers, Joseph, Esq.
* Roxburgh, Duke of, 2 Copies
Rudge, Miss

* Salisbury, the Lord Bishop of
* Scudamore, Mrs. A. Hereford, 5 Copies
Shedden, Robert, Esq.
Shee, George, Esq.
Shee, Martin Arthur. Esq. A. R. A.
Sheffield, Lord
Shield, William, Esq.
Skipsey, William, Esq. R. N.
* Smith, Sir John, Bart.
Sneyd, Rev. William
Sneyd, Rev. Thomas, Ballyborough
Sneyd, Nathaniel, Esq.
Spear, Miss, Ballyborough
Steell, Robert, Esq.
* Steers, J. W. Esq.
* Steers, Charles, Esq. 2 Copies
* Steers, Edward, Esq.
Stepple, Henry, Esq.
Still, Robert, Esq.
Still, Rev. John
Stokes, John, Esq.
Story, Rev. Joseph
Story, Rev. Edward
Story, Miss Anna
* Sumner, Rev. Dr. Provost of King's College, Cambridge, 2 Copies
Sumner, Rev. Mr. Fellow of King's College, Cambridge

Swale, John, Esq.
Swale, Mrs. C.
Swale, Miss F.

* Tate, George, Esq. 2 Copies
* Tate, Mrs. Grosvenor Place, 2 Copies
* Tate, Miss, 2 Copies
* Tate, Rev. Benjamin
Tatlow, Miss Mary
Tatlow, Miss Charlotte
Tatlow, Master John
* Thompson, Henry, Esq.
Thurlow, Miss
* Tighe, R. S. Esq.
Turner, Rev. J. D. D. Dean of Nor-
wich

Vaughan, William, Esq.

* Walpole, Lord
* Warren, Peter, Esq. 2 Copies
* Warren, John Willing, Esq.
* Waters, Mrs. Bath
Wheelwright, Charles Apthorpe, Esq.
* Whitbread, Samuel, Esq. 5 Copies
* White, Mr. Bookseller, 9 Copies
Winder, Miss, Putney
Wood, George, Esq.
* Woodward, Mr. Bath
Woodward, Miss, Bath
* Wray, Mrs. Richmond, 2 Copies

Young, John, Esq.

ANECDOTES

OF

GEORGE FREDERICK HANDEL.

ANECDOTES

GEORGE FREDERICK HANDEL.

I T has been a long received opinion, that the offspring of persons advanced in years are generally weak in frame as well as intellect, and evidently show the languor of the stock from which they sprung; but George Frederick Handel, the subject of the present Memoirs, is a strong instance that such conclusions are not founded in truth: for though his father at the time of his birth was sixty-one years of age, his son astonished the world as an uncommon example of early approach to excellence, great strength of constitution, and continued abilities.

Handel was born on the 24th of February, 1686, at Hall, a city in the dutchy of Magdeburg, in the circle of Upper Saxony, where his father resided as a physician. He was the child of a second marriage. His father destined him to the profession of the civil law; but Handel discovered in his early childhood a strong passion for music.

Few instances occur of a more early, decided, or fortunate propensity to a particular science.   Pope said of himself that

" He lisp'd in numbers, and the numbers came ;"

Handel, though he never possessed a fine voice, could sing as soon as he could speak, and evinced such a predilection for music, that the father carefully kept out of his reach all instruments, with the hopes of weaning his mind from what he deemed a degrading attachment.   But the child contrived to obtain possession of a clavicord, which he secreted in the garret, and at night, when he was supposed to be asleep, the young enthusiast was awake; and the imagination may fondly view him striking the strings of his lyre,—that lyre which was to charm all Europe with its energy.

It is the property of Genius to possess that inflexible spirit, and unalterable adherence to a resolution once formed, which defies opposition, diminishes danger, and surmounts impediment : this disposition tyrannically checked, preys on the temper, and settles into gloominess and misanthropy ; but if cherished, and warmed with moderate success, it produces the noblest and most expansive efforts of human energy.   This disposition was the characteristic of Handel ; and his inflexible spirit of perseverance is marked by a trivial occurrence, which took place in the seventh year of his age.   His father, purposing to visit one of his sons, who was valet de chambre to the Duke of Saxe Weisenfeld, Handel earnestly intreated that he might be allowed to accompany him ; but his request was peremptorily rejected.   The father set off in a chaise ; and when he had travelled a few miles, he was surprised at the sight of his son, who, with a strength greatly surpassing his years, had set out on foot and overtaken the carriage, the progress of which had been retarded by the badness of the roads. After a sharp animadversion, and some reluctance, the little suppliant was permitted to take his seat, and gratify his earnest desire of visiting his brother.

At the Duke's court, Handel was not so closely watched by his father, as at home. He enjoyed many opportunities of indulging his natural propensity; and he contrived, occasionally, to play upon the organ in the Duke's chapel at the conclusion of divine service. One morning the Duke hearing the organ touched in an unusual manner, inquired of his valet who was the performer. The valet replied that it was his brother; and mentioning at the same time his wonderful talents and predilection for music, and his father's repugnance, the Duke sent for them both. After other inquiries, the Duke was so much pleased with the spirit and talents of the boy, that he pleaded the cause of nature: he represented it as a crime against the public and posterity, to rob the world of such a genius; and, finally, persuaded the father to sacrifice his own scruples, and to permit his son to be instructed in the profession for which he had evinced so strong an inclination. A more interesting scene can hardly be conceived, than Handel listening to the arguments of his powerful advocate, and marking his final triumph over the reluctant prejudices of his parent. The Duke became so much interested in his success, that, at his departure, he made him a present, and promised his protection if he zealously applied to his studies.

At his return to Hall, his father placed him under the tuition of William Zackau, organist to the cathedral; a man of science and judgment. Zackau carefully instilled into his scholar, a thorough knowledge of the principles of harmony, and by explaining to him the different styles of Italian and German composition, he laid the foundation of that fame, which was to claim so distinguished a place in the annals of music. Handel made so rapid a progress, that before he had completed his seventh year, he was able to officiate on the organ for his master; and at the age of nine, he began to study composition. At this early period of his life he is said to have composed, every week, during three successive years, a spiritual cantata, or church service for voices, with instrumental accompaniments.*

Having exhausted his source of improvement at Hall, he became desirous of enlarging his knowledge, and was eager to obtain applause on a more distinguished theatre. He made choice of Berlin as the

* It has long been a matter of curious research among the admirers of Handel, to discover any traces of his early studies. Among Mr. Smith's collection of music, now in the possession of his daughter-in-law, Lady Rivers, is a book of manuscript music, dated 1698, and inscribed with the initials G. F. H. It was evidently a common-place book belonging to Handel in the fourteenth year of his age. The greater part is in his own hand, and the notes are characterized by a peculiar manner of forming the crotchets.

It contains various airs, choruses, capricios, fugues, and other pieces of music, with the names of contemporary musicians, such as Zackau, Alberti, Frobergher, Krieger, Kerl, Ebner, Strunch. They were probably exercises adopted at pleasure, or dictated for him to work upon, by his master. The composition is uncommonly scientific, and contains the seeds of many of his subsequent performances.

Sir John Hawkins says, that at the age of *nine*, Handel composed motetts for the service of the church, and continued to make one every week for three years. *Hist. of* spot, where the Opera, under the patronage of Frederick the First, was in a flourishing state, and boasted the aid of the most distinguished musicians of Italy; among whom Buononcini and Attilio were not the least conspicuous. The fame of Handel had preceded him; but these two musicians considered him a mere child, whose abilities had been greatly exaggerated: Buononcini, therefore, in order to try his skill, composed a cantata in the chromatic style, in which he comprized difficulties sufficient to puzzle an experienced master. Handel, however, treated this formidable composition as a mere trifle; he executed it at sight, with a degree of accuracy, truth, and expression, hardly to be expected from repeated practice, and from an aged performer.

But the display of congenial powers, did not impress Buononcini with one sentiment of friendship, or draw from him any symptom of kindness; though civil, he behaved to Handel with such reserve, as seemed to imply, that the foundation of future animosity was laid at that moment. Attilio, on the contrary, shewed him a partiality; the result of a generous and honourable disposition. He would place him for hours at his harpsichord, and was anxious to aid his progress in composition, or facilitate his readiness in execution.

Music. Dr. Burney observes, that when only ten years old, Handel composed a set of Sonatas in three parts. It seems as if they were published. He adds, that " Lord Marchmont picked them up in his travels, and that they are now in the King's Collection." The exercises to which Handel was accustomed, observes Sir John Hawkins, were compositions and fugues upon airs, or subjects delivered to him from time to time by his master. He adds, this is the mode of exercise for young proficients in music, and is also the test of a master.

Proud to patronize so promising a genius, Frederick frequently invited him to court, made him considerable presents, and, finally, proposed to send him to Italy at his own charge. This proposal Handel was eager to accept; but his father, foreseeing that it would impose a restraint on his son, declined; alleging as an excuse, that his very advanced age required his son's presence. In compliance with his father's injunctions Handel left Berlin, unwilling to expose himself to further solicitation.

Though Handel perfectly acquiesced in the propriety of the motives which induced his father to reject the proposal of Frederick, yet the flattering reception he had met with in his two excursions from home, opened to his view the fairest prospects of profit and celebrity. His father dying, a diminution in his mother's income induced him to repair to Hamburgh, where the Opera was next in repute to that of Berlin. On his arrival he secured an engagement at the opera-house, not as a principal performer on the harpsichord, but as second ripieno violin. So extraordinary a step of voluntary self-abasement will appear singular; but it was the effect of a principle unbecoming the dignity of a great mind, which led him to affect a simplicity, or rather humility of conduct, founded on vanity, and which his youth only could excuse, that he might enjoy the surprise excited by an unexpected display of his powers. Such an opportunity soon occurred. Reinhard Keiser, the leader of the band, encumbered with debts, was obliged to absent himself; and to the general astonishment, the unobserved performer on the violin took his seat before the harpsichord, and soon convinced his audience, and the band, that they had no reason to regret, but ought to exult in the change.

There is a received account of a contest for this enviable precedence, and an attempt to assassinate Handel, which was founded on a misrepresentation of the following occurrence. Matheson, who was afterwards Secretary to the English Resident, and wrote several books on the subject of Music, was at that time a principal singer, and occasional composer. He had set to music the opera of Cleopatra, in which he himself performed Antony; but his part being over in an early period of the piece, it was his custom to take his seat at the harpsichord, and conduct the band during the rest of the performance. This had been submitted to by Keiser; but Handel was not of a disposition so accommodating. He refused to resign his seat; and Matheson, in a rage, as they were going down the steps of the orchestra at the close of the opera, gave him a blow. Their swords were instantly drawn; but Matheson's weapon fortunately breaking against his antagonist's button, put an end to the rencounter. They had been in habits of intimacy, which they soon resumed; and were rejoiced at the lucky conclusion of so serious an incident, arising from so trifling a cause.

In addition to the profits of his engagement, Handel had scholars sufficient to render all assistance from his mother unnecessary; and he returned the first remittance she sent him, with a supply from his savings. Before his quarrel with Matheson, he had travelled with him to Lubeck, where there was a vacancy for the organist's place. They performed this journey in the public caravan, with all the thoughtless hilarity of youth, singing extempore duets, and amusing themselves with all imaginable frolics on the road; to which the affected simplicity and archness of Handel gave an exquisite zest. Finding the acceptance of the place coupled with a condition, that the organist was to take a wife, who was to be chosen for him by the magistrates, they each of them declined offering themselves on such conditions, and returned together to Hamburgh.

During his residence at Hamburgh, he composed his first Italian opera of Almira (1704). It met with great and flattering success, and ran thirty nights without intermission. The next year he produced Nerone; and the two succeeding years Florindo, and Dafne; all which were eminently successful. But he was at this time so much engaged with his scholars, and in the production of lessons for the harpsichord, that he did not give to the public so many operas as the fertility of his genius would have enabled him.

At this period the Prince of Tuscany, brother to the Grand Duke, came to Hamburgh, and engaged Handel's attention, by introducing to his notice a considerable variety of Italian music; dwelling with patriotic enthusiasm on the pre-eminence of his countrymen. He lamented that Handel had not visited a region, where every branch of the musical science was carried to the highest perfection, and offered his patronage if he would accompany him to Florence. Though Handel had been long desirous of going to Italy, he politely declined this offer, from a noble spirit of independence, which was never known to forsake him, even in the most distressful seasons of his life. But his visit was only postponed.

Having acquired a sufficient sum to defray his expences, he left Hamburgh in 1708, and repaired to Florence; where his reception was

such as might be expected from the countenance of the exalted per-
sonage who introduced him. At Florence he composed the opera of
Rodrigo, for which the Grand Duke presented him an hundred sequins,
and a service of plate. From Florence he proceeded to Venice, where
he arrived *incognito* at the Carnival, and was immediately discovered
by Scarlatti, who, listening to him as he sat at the harpsichord in his
visor, exclaimed, that the performer must be either the famous Saxon,
or the devil.

(1709.) He was soon prevailed upon to compose the opera of
Agrippina, and he effected it in three weeks, to the astonishment of
Venice; and, as the author of so excellent and unexpected a performance, he was almost idolized. Agrippina was brought out at a theatre
which had been shut up for a considerable time, but which was now
crowded every night; and all the first singers from the other theatres
offered to perform in the opera of *Il caro Sassone.* The audience
knew no bounds in testifying their admiration. Vittoria, an excellent
actress, singer, and favourite mistress of the Grand Duke of Tuscany,
who had conceived an affection for Handel at Florence, came to Venice,
and bore a principal part in the new opera. His youth and comeliness,
joined to his musical fame, had made an impression on her heart; but
Handel was too prudent to encourage an attachment, which might
have occasioned the ruin of both.

From Venice he went to Rome, preceded by his illustrious reputation, which procured him the immediate patronage of Cardinal
Ottoboni; for whom he composed several pieces in so masterly a style,
as astonished, and even confounded the oldest proficients. He had

trials of skill with eminent musicians, particularly with *Dominico Scarlatti*, who had the honour, in some measure, to divide the laurel with him; for though Handel was allowed a distinguished superiority on the organ, yet, on the harpsichord, the contest remained doubtful. Handel was also courted by Cardinals Pamfilio and Colonna. For Cardinal Pamfilio, who possessed the talent of making extempore poetry, Handel composed extempore music. Among these were *Il Trionfo del Tempo*, and a poem in praise of the Musician, wherein Pamfilio compared him to Orpheus.

From Rome he proceeded to Naples, where he was no less the object of esteem and admiration; and at the request of Donna Laura, a Spanish princess, he composed *Acige e Galatea*.* He then made a second visit to Florence, Rome, and Venice, and at length resolved to quit Italy, where his reputation had acquired a lustre exceeding his most sanguine expectations. He was distinguished, according to the custom of the country, by the appellation of *Il Sassone;* and had he remained in Italy, that distinction would have superseded his patronimic. Though his productions at the time were numerous, few are now extant, except the pieces which have been alluded to.

After his return to Germany, (1710) he visited Hanover. Steffani, a learned and elegant composer, whom he had known at Venice, and who was a great favourite at the Electoral court, introduced him to the notice of the Princess Sophia, and her grandson the Electoral

---

* This was totally different from the serenata written by Gay, and so well known in England. The Italian names of Handel's operas are generally preserved in his Life, to distinguish them from his English compositions.

Prince, afterwards George the Second. Baron Kilmanseg, who had been acquainted with him in Italy, recommended him to the attention of the Elector, afterwards George the First; who, struck with his merit, proposed to retain him in his service, with a salary of fifteen hundred crowns per annum. This liberal offer Handel accepted; but on condition, that he should be permitted to visit England, whither he had been invited by many persons of high rank, whom he had seen in Italy, and at Hanover. The Elector agreed to these conditions; and afterwards, by the friendly interference of Steffani, appointed him master of the chapel. In his way to England he visited his native city, where he paid his duty to his mother, who was blind and infirm, and renewed his intimacy with his relations and friends, amongst whom Zackau was not forgotten. At Dusseldorf he had a flattering reception from the Elector Palatine, who presented him with a service of plate, and wished to retain him in his Court.

In England, (1710) observes Dr. Burney, his reception was as flattering to himself, as honourable to the nation; at this time no less successful in war than in the cultivation of the arts of peace. To the wit, poetry, literature, and science, which marked this period of our history, Handel added all the blandishments of a nervous and learned music, which he first brought hither, planted, and lived to see grow to a very flourishing state. The impatience of the public was so great, that Handel was immediately employed in setting to music the opera of Rinaldo, which was prepared and finished with unparalleled haste. Aaron Hill, who was manager of the opera, sketched the plan from Tasso's *Gierusalemme Liberata,* and Rossi, the Italian poet, composed the drama. In his Preface, Rossi commends Handel's musical talents in the highest strain of panegyric, and calls him the Orpheus of the age. He observes, that Handel scarcely allowed him time to write the words; and that, to his great astonishment, he set the whole to music in the short space of a fortnight. The principal part was written for Nicolini, whose graceful and expressive action was praised by Steele, in the Tatler.* Rinaldo was received with the greatest applause, not only on its first appearance, but on three subsequent revivals; and Walsh, the music seller, is reputed to have gained fifteen hundred pounds by printing the scores.

Having staid in England near a twelvemonth, during which his execution was no less admired than his compositions, Handel took leave of Queen Anne, who accompanied several valuable presents with expressions of regret at his departure, and wishes for his speedy return; which he respectfully promised should take place as soon as he could obtain permission of the Elector.

On his arrival at Hanover, Handel composed twelve chamber duets, and a few other pieces of little importance; and soon obtained permission to return to England, on the positive assurance that he would not long absent himself from the Electoral dominions. His return to London was hailed by the musical world as a national acquisition, and every measure was adopted to render his abode pleasant and permanent. An eminent occasion was not long wanting for the full exercise of his great talents. He was called upon to compose the Grand Jubilate, and Te Deum, for the conclusion of the peace of Utrecht. In that composition he acquitted himself with all that wonderful effect

* No. 115.

of sublimity and judgment, for which he was remarkable. He also composed for the Opera-house, Teseo, and Il Pastor Fido; and both operas were well received. The Queen was so captivated with his performances, that she settled on him an annual pension of two hundred pounds, and the nobility vied with each other in proving their esteem for so distinguished a musician; who, thus rewarded, courted, and patronized, forgot his promise of returning to Germany.

In 1714 Queen Anne died. The accession of his liberal patron, who, under the title of George the First, succeeded to the throne, under other circumstances would have been the moment of exultation; but instead of appearing in the foremost rank of congratulators, Handel did not venture to present himself at Court. From this embarrassment, however, he was happily relieved by the kindness of Baron Kilmanseg, Master of the Horse to George the First as Elector of Hanover. Apprized that his Majesty had projected a party on the Thames, he informed Handel of the King's intention: Handel immediately produced that celebrated composition, known by the title of the Water Music. Having procured a band, he followed the barge, and watching his opportunity, unexpectedly charmed the Royal party by melodies of singular effect and sweetness. The King inquiring who was the composer of that exquisite harmony, Baron Kilmanseg said that it was Handel; stated his contrition, and sued for his restoration to favour. This respectful attempt at reconciliation, and atonement for his conduct, mollified the Sovereign. Soon afterwards, Geminiani was commanded to play, in the King's closet, twelve solos which he had recently composed: fearful that their proper effect would be lost by an indifferent accompaniment, he expressed a wish that Handel might be permitted to preside at the harpsichord. This request was conveyed to the King, and enforced by the friendly solicitation of the Baron. Handel was restored to favour; and the King increased the pension granted by Queen Anne to four hundred pounds a year.

In the course of the summer, Handel passed several months at Barn Elms, in Surrey, with Mr. Andrews; and in the winter, at that gentleman's house in town. He was also invited (1715) to the mansion of the Earl of Burlington, where he composed Amadige, or Amadis de Gaul; the only opera of his which appeared (May 15,) on the boards of the King's Theatre for five years. He remained three years with Lord Burlington, during which time he became acquainted with Pope, Gay, and Arbuthnot. Pope not only had no knowledge of the science of music, but received no gratification from " the concord of sweet sounds." He heard the performances of Handel with perfect indifference, if not impatience. Gay was pleased with music without understanding it, but forgot the performance when the notes ceased to vibrate. Arbuthnot, on the contrary, who was a judge of music, and a composer, felt the merits of Handel, and conceived an esteem for him, which he afterwards displayed under the most trying circumstances. From the Earl of Burlington's, Handel went to Cannons, the seat of the Duke of Chandos, where he remained two years as composer for the chapel; producing numerous anthems and other sacred pieces, and the English serenata of Acis and Galatea.

During the last year (1720) of his residence at Cannons, the principal nobility and gentry resolved to establish an Academy of Music. The King was the patron, and subscribed one thousand pounds; and the whole subscription amounted to fifty thousand pounds. Application being made to Handel to assume the management, he consented; and, having set off for Dresden to procure singers, returned with Senesino, and several other performers, prepared to open the Opera-house in a style of superior splendour. He first produced for the Academy the Opera of Radamisto; the great success of which evinced his talents as a composer, and a happy power of adapting airs to the abilities of the respective singers. Radamisto proved as great a favourite in London, as Agrippina had proved at Venice; and disappointed crowds went every night from the house, unable to obtain seats. The great success of Handel did not, however, exempt him from the rivalship of Buononcini and Attilio. They had been invited to England by the former managers of the Opera; and as they were composers of acknowledged merit, their admirers refused to concede the precedence to Handel. Hence arose those musical feuds, which Swift has ridiculed as a dispute,

" 'Twixt Tweedle-dum, and Tweedle-dee,"

and which were brought to a crisis in the succeeding winter. It was agreed by the friends of the three rivals, that each of them should compose an act of the Opera of Mutius Scævola, and an overture. Buononcini set the first act, Attilio the second, and Handel the third. The preference was given to Handel; he was appointed composer; the Academy was finally established, and the Opera prosperously conducted during nine years.

During this period he composed fifteen Operas, all of which possessed extraordinary merit, and were highly successful; but either from mismanagement in the pecuniary concerns of the house, or from

D

the impossibility of supporting an Opera in London, without constant contributions, the condition of the treasury became so unprosperous, that the whole sum subscribed, was in this short and brilliant period entirely exhausted, and the Academy dissolved. This is the real cause of the termination of this splendid undertaking, though it has been ignorantly ascribed to the irritability of Handel. It is true, indeed, that the composer was not of a temper to treat singers with great respect ; he considered them, perhaps too much, as mere instruments, which gave utterance to that harmony, of which he was so distinguished an Author. He possessed the impetuosity and inflexibility of genius. On the contrary, Senesino, intoxicated with popular applause, which his talents well merited, did not bend with implicit submission to the wishes of the manager. Disputes certainly ran high between Handel and Senesino, before the dissolution of the Academy; but it is not true, that their irreconcilable antipathy was the occasion of that event. Senesino sung in operas composed by Handel, and under his management, two years after the dissolution had taken place.

If Handel was little disposed to submit to the caprice of the male performers, he was not of a temper patiently to endure the disturbance arising from female squabbles for precedence; and still less, to have his views thwarted by their peevishness, or non-compliance with rules which he had thought necessary to prescribe. His choler on such occasions surmounted all bounds of discretion. When Cuzzoni had refused to sing an air which he had composed for her, he exclaimed in a rage, that he well knew that she had the spirit of a devil; but that he would convince her whom she had to deal with, in dealing with him, for that he was Beelzebub, the Prince of the Devils; and seizing her by the waist, threatened to throw her from the window, if she persisted in her refusal. The pride and haughtiness of Cuzzoni, and Faustina, was of that description, that neither of them would sing when the other was present; and persons of the first distinction humoured this insolence, by enlisting in parties, and degrading themselves by the most unworthy condescensions. But their quarrels with Handel had little effect to the prejudice of the Academy, for Cuzzoni sung for him at the same time with Senesino.

At the close of the last season (1728) of the Academy, the singers dispersed, and during a whole year there was no Italian Opera in London. In this interval, Handel being determined, in conjunction with Heidegger, to establish Operas on their private account, went to Italy in search of performers. He returned (1729) with a respectable band, and opened the house (29th December) with Lotario; which, together with Parthenope, were sufficient attractions for the season. The following year, Senesino sung for him in various Operas, and continued to perform till Handel's dissensions with him and Cuzzoni became so violent, that they could no longer remain united.

An opposition was immediately excited by many persons of distinction, who had taken umbrage that they were excluded from their subscription boxes; and that the price of admission was raised to a guinea when Oratorios were performed. These imprudent measures gave birth to a rival Opera, at the theatre in Lincoln's Inn Fields; which was patronized by many persons of quality, and to which several of the singers and instrumental performers, whom Handel had engaged, deserted. Senesino complained that Handel no longer composed for him in his usual style; he therefore quitted his theatre, and Cuzzoni accompanied him.

Handel, however, was not to be intimidated. Carestini, Strada, the Negri family, Durastanti, and Scalzi, still remained; and he possessed that powerful resource which never failed him, his own immeasurable abilities. It is not intended to describe the progress of this contest, which ruined Handel's finances, impaired his health, and even affected his understanding. He fought manfully, changed alternately to the Haymarket, Lincoln's Inn Fields, and Covent Garden Theatre, varying his performers, and even his style of music. Yet such was the inveteracy of the opposing party, that though his Operas were most admirable compositions, and those of his adversaries far inferior in merit, the tide of fashion set decidedly against him.

In this arduous situation, which lasted near eleven years, he displayed great superiority and force of mind. He did not condescend to conciliate favour by degrading concession, or to reduce the expence, by engaging inferior performers, or diminishing the salaries of those whom he employed. On the contrary, his band was always numerous, well selected, and liberally paid; but so long a contest, with such expensive exertions and such unfavourable consequences, could not fail alike to injure the body and the mind. Handel evinced, in the course of the struggle, occasional symptoms of mental derangement, and lost the use of his right arm by a stroke of the palsy. Suffering under this affliction, he went immediately to Tunbridge, and from thence to Aix-la-Chapelle.

In the days of his prosperity he had invested a considerable sum in the funds; but at the end of this pertinacious opposition he had lost ten thousand pounds, the produce of his youthful exertions, and was besides so greatly in debt, that he was in daily fear of being arrested for the salaries of his performers; with whom, however, he contrived to settle by bonds, which were afterwards duly discharged. It is not the least astonishing part of his character, that his promptitude of invention, and brilliancy of ideas, in all this time did not forsake him. At the moment of his recovery (1737) from a violent illness, and even attended with fits of lunacy, his faculties were exerted with their full vigour in bringing forward the Opera of Faramond; and in composing the funeral anthem on the death of his lamented patroness, Queen Caroline, equal in pathos and sublimity to his best compositions.

Nor had his enemies any cause to exult. Though Handel gave up the contest, no victory was gained by them; though he was impoverished, they were not enriched. It is clearly ascertained, that without considerable subscriptions, great abilities in the composers, excellence in the singers, and strenuous exertions, an Opera can never be advantageously maintained in London. When all the patronage and the best singers were enlisted on one side, and the best composers on the other, it was easy to suppose that both undertakings would fail. The public always sided with Handel; but the public, except of the higher class of society, are not sufficiently attached to the Italian Opera, to give celebrity and profit to the undertaking. To be sensible of the beauties of Italian music, requires an intimacy with the science, and a knowledge of the language. Few possess those advantages. The language of Nature is open to all, whether in expression or action; but the grace of expression and action is not sufficient to engage the attention of mankind, where sense is concealed by an unknown idiom, and the understanding is not gratified by a perception of appropriate harmony.

Handel could not complain of neglect. Though Farinelli and the nobility at that time opposed him; though he had no capital singer except Strada, and laboured under other disadvantages, his Alexander's Feast (19th February, 1736) was attended by an audience uncommonly numerous. Thirteen hundred persons were assembled at the Theatre of Covent Garden, and the receipt of the house amounted to four hundred and fifty pounds. His benefit at the Haymarket, in the following month (28th March, 1738), was equally well attended; the pit was laid into boxes, and the house crowded in every part. He received an honourable mark of distinction from the liberality of an individual, seldom conferred on any man during his life. His statue, admirably sculptured by Roubillac, was placed by Mr. Jonathan Tyers in the gardens at Vauxhall (1738); and the public coincided in the justice and propriety of the compliment paid to his merit.

It may be alleged, in contradiction to Handel's popularity, that several of his Operas, published in this interval by subscription, barely defrayed the expences; but it is to be observed, that the most important and beneficial class of subscribers, were adverse to his interests; and that the number of rival composers who advanced their claims to the patronage of the public, though they could not contest the palm, interfered and lessened his profits.

At length (1741) Handel determined to abandon Opera compositions. He had already produced thirty-nine Operas for the English stage; all excellent, and possessing that infinite variety, which his musical talents were capable of producing. His last Opera was Deidamia; which, though abounding in beauties, was received with indifference, and performed but three nights. The flattering reception which Handel had met with when he visited Oxford, where he was offered the degree of Doctor in Music, but declined accepting it, induced him to try the event of a journey to Ireland. He was received at Dublin with such strong marks of approbation, as did no less honour to him, than to the taste of the nation. His Messiah, which was reported to have been coldly received in London, * was applauded with all the enthusiasm due to claims of such uncommon excellence. He remained in Ireland about nine months, and acquired every advantage which health, fame, and profit, could bestow. The public in his absence had become fully sensible of his merits; Arbuthnot had ever been his friend, and written pamphlets in his favour, while the opposition against him was in its full force; Pope, more economical of praise, now ventured that compliment in the Dunciad, which acknowledges his title to musical fame; and Handel no longer had to contend with prejudices, or combat the malignancy of inveterate opposition.

As from this period Handel must be considered as the composer of Oratorios, it will be proper to give a short account of their rise and progress. His first Oratorio was Esther; which was composed

---

* Dr. Burney has been at the laudable pains to disprove the fact, and has succeeded in rendering it doubtful.

in 1720, for the Duke of Chandos, at Cannons; but was not given to the public till eleven years after, when it was performed by the children of the King's chapel. The chorus was sung after the manner of the ancients, and the singers were placed between the stage and the orchestra. The instrumental performers were, principally, gentlemen belonging to the Philharmonic Society. This novel species of entertainment was so greatly approved, that the representation was repeated at the Crown and Anchor. Their success inspired Handel with new hopes. Esther was again performed at the Haymarket, in 1733: it ran ten nights; and with the addition of Handel's concertos on the organ, then new to the public, proved sufficiently attractive. He next produced Deborah: and in his journey to Oxford in the same year, Athalia. In the succeeding year he revived Acis and Galatea, set to music Alexander's Feast, Israel in Egypt, L'Allegro ed il Penseroso, Saul, and the Messiah.

After his return from Ireland, he continued every year the same style of composition, and generally with the greatest success; though with occasional failures, owing to the latent seeds of former animosity. His merit and perseverance were amply rewarded; he retained a firm hold of the public favour and patronage to the end of his life; and he was not only enabled to clear himself from all incumbrances, but to realize a fortune of twenty thousand pounds.

Some years before his death (1751), he was afflicted with a gutta serena, which, as he justly apprehended, in the end deprived him of sight; though he underwent the operation of couching. His spirits for a short time sunk under this affliction; but when he found the

evil incurable, he submitted with resignation. Unable without assistance to conduct the Oratorios, he applied to his pupil and long-
tried friend Mr. Smith, and by his assistance they were continued.

It was a most affecting spectacle to see the venerable musician,
whose efforts had charmed the ear of a discerning public, led by the
hand of friendship to the front of the stage, to make an obeisance of
acknowledgment to his enraptured audience.

When Handel became blind, though he no longer presided over
the Oratorios, he still introduced concertos on the organ between the
acts. At first he relied on his memory, but the exertion becoming
painful to him, he had recourse to the inexhaustible stores of his rich
and fertile imagination. He gave to the band, only such parts of his
intended composition, as were to be filled up by their accompaniment;
and relied on his own powers of invention to produce, at the impulse
of the moment, those captivating passages, which arrested attention,
and enchanted his auditors.

It is curious, though painful to a thinking mind, to trace the com-
parison between Homer, Milton, and Handel; all of them deprived of
sight, and each exerting his faculties under that severe visitation, to
the wonder of an admiring world. The singular and sublime talents
of Milton, displayed in his Paradise Lost, were better known indeed
to posterity, than to his contemporaries. The merits of that animated
composition, were gradually unfolded; but the Grecian Bard sang
his Iliad and Odyssey amidst the praises of his admiring countrymen.
Handel though a foreigner, yet with talents equally sublime, and

melody not inferior, heard his own fame resounded in the loud tribute of deserved commendation.

Nature at last became exhausted, he exhibited evident symptoms of decay; his appetite failed him, and he saw without dismay his dissolution approaching. But his extraordinary faculties continued to the end of his life: his last public performance (6th April, 1759) took place only a week before he died (14th April); and that great event happened, as he had often expressed his earnest wish, on Good Friday. He was buried in Westminster Abbey; his funeral sermon was preached by Dr. Pearce, Bishop of Rochester; and at his own expence a marble monument was erected to his memory, by the sculpture of Roubillac. His figure is represented standing before the organ, and listening to the harp of an Angel. On a scroll are recorded his own divine notes, set to those emphatical words, comprising the sum of Christian hope, " I know that my Redeemer liveth."

George Frederick Handel, was seventy-three years of age when he died. He was large in person, and his natural corpulency, which increased as he advanced in life, rendered his whole appearance of that bulky proportion, as to give rise to Quin's inelegant, but forcible expression; that his hands were feet, and his fingers toes. From a sedentary life, he had contracted a stiffness in his joints, which in addition to his great weight and weakness of body, rendered his gait awkward; still his countenance was open, manly, and animated; expressive of all that grandeur and benevolence, which were the prominent features of his character. In temper he was irascible, impatient of contradiction, but not vindictive; jealous of his musical

pre-eminence, and tenacious in all points, which regarded his professional honour.

He was averse to all restraint on his freedom. Being informed at
the Spa, that the King of Prussia was expected, and purposed to be
witness of his musical powers, to the great disappointment of the
monarch, he quitted the place some days before his arrival; unwilling to expose himself to solicitations he had determined not to
comply with, or to commands which he could not resist. In England
he was always well received and warmly patronized; but his general
aversion to subscription engagements, and the resolute inflexibility of
his temper, prevented the accession of some friends, and alienated
others. With conscious pride, he was unwilling to be indebted but to
his own abilities for his advancement, and they finally triumphed over
all his opposers.

His chief foible was a culpable indulgence in the sensual gratifications of the table; but this foible was amply compensated by a
sedulous attention to every religious duty, and moral obligation. His
understanding was excellent, and his knowledge extensive. Besides
the German, his native tongue, he was intimate with the English, and
master of the Latin, French, and Italian languages : he had acquired
a taste for painting, which he improved during his residence in Italy,
and felt great pleasure in contemplating the works of art. His great
delight was derived from his attachment to his own science, and he
experienced particular satisfaction from religious principles, in presiding
at the organ in the cathedral church of St. Paul. He frequently declared in conversation, the high gratification he enjoyed in setting the

Scriptures to music, and how greatly he was edified by contemplating the sublime passages abounding in the sacred writings.

From the same motive he was regular in his attendance on divine service, at his parish church near Hanover Square, where his devout posture of humility, and earnestness of voice and gesture, avowing his faith, acknowledging his errors, and appealing to his Maker for mercy, were strongly impressive.

Handel contracted few intimacies, and when his early friends died, he was not solicitous of acquiring new ones. He was never married; but his celibacy must not be attributed to any deficiency of personal attractions, or to the source which Sir John Hawkins unjustly supposes, the want of social affection. On the contrary, it was owing to the independency of his disposition, which feared degradation, and dreaded confinement. For when he was young, two of his scholars, ladies of considerable fortune, were so much enamoured of him, that each was desirous of a matrimonial alliance. The first is said to have fallen a victim to her attachment. Handel would have married her; but his pride was stung by the coarse declaration of her mother, that she never would consent to the marriage of her daughter with a fiddler; and, in-dignant at the expression, he declined all further intercourse. After the death of the mother, the father renewed the acquaintance, and informed him that all obstacles were removed; but he replied, that the time was now past; and the young lady fell into a decline, which soon terminated her existence. The second attachment, was a lady splendidly related, whose hand he might have obtained by renouncing his profession. That condition he resolutely refused, and laudably declined the connection which was to prove a restriction on the great faculties of his mind.

Handel's religious disposition was not a mere display, it was amply productive of religion's best fruit, charity; and this liberal sentiment not only influenced him in the day of prosperity, but even when standing on the very brink of ruin. He performed Acis and Galatea (1740), for the benefit of the musical fund: the next year he gave them his Epithalamium, called *Parnasso in Festa*, and further extended his kindness by a legacy of one thousand pounds. He was no less bountiful to the Foundling Hospital; his early exertions in its favour were the principal support of that respectable establishment. He gave an organ to the chapel; and an annual benefit, by which seven thousand pounds was cleared in the course of a few years. He also presented the governors with the original score of the Messiah. His charity was by no means restricted to public donations, he was equally attentive to the claims of friendship, affection, and gratitude. The widow of his master Zackau, being old and poor, received from him frequent remittances; and her son would have enjoyed the benefits of his liberality; but for his profligacy, and incurable drunkenness. The bulk of Handel's fortune was bequeathed to his relations. All his music he left to Mr. Smith.

There is not any circumstance more delightful to the eye of contemplation, than to observe great talents exerted in the cause of benevolence and humanity. Mason has most beautifully described its effects upon the mind.—

" Humanity, thy awful strain shall greet the ear
    " Sonorous, sweet, and clear.
" And as amidst the dulcet notes that breathe
        " From flute or lyre,
" The deep base rolls its manly melody,
        " Guiding the tuneful choir:
    " So thou, Humanity, shalt lead along
    " The accordant passions in this moral song,
" And give one mental concert, truest harmony."

To the literary world he owed little obligation. Arbuthnot, indeed, was his friend. Pope, notwithstanding his high compliment, slighted, and Swift ridiculed him: but that patronage, which had first reflected favour, and conferred honour on him, was the countenance shewn to him by the illustrious house of Brunswick. George the First had settled on him a pension of £200. a year, in addition to that already granted by Anne; George the Second added a pension of equal amount, in reward for teaching the Royal Children; these munificent donations formed his support in the hour of his adversity, and the habit of confining his expences adhered to him through life. He frequently presided at those concerts which were held in the royal library, and was remarkable for enforcing decorum and attention; though the performers, and the audience, were persons of the first distinction. The King, and Prince and Princess of Wales, were ever fond of his music, and attended his Oratorios, even when they were so much deserted, that Lord Chesterfield wittily, but ill naturedly called attending an oratorio, " an intrusion on his Majesty's privacy."

His own death deprived him of the patronage which would have resulted from the acknowledged taste of the present Sovereign. But it ought not, in the life of Handel, to be omitted, that, though that gratification was denied, the British Monarch presided at the Commemoration of Handel; the most splendid tribute ever paid to posthumous fame.

In the same Abbey where his body lies interred, those anthems which he had composed for the funeral service of Queen Caroline, together with the most celebrated pieces of his compositions, were judiciously selected for the celebration of his own memory; and performed in the highest style of instrumental perfection and vocal excellence. It was an honour to the profession, to the nation, and to the Sovereign.

The genius and abilities of Handel, were truly gigantic, and Pope justly said of him,

" Strong in new arms the giant Handel stands,
" Like bold Briareus with a hundred hands."

No species of composition escaped him; the wonderful force of his execution was as astonishing as the vast efforts of his mind. He made the organ his own instrument; and Scarlatti declared, that, till he heard Handel, he had no conception of his powers. Akenside, in delineating the character of Shakspeare remarks, that

" Different minds
" Incline to different objects:—one pursues

" The vast alone, the wonderful, the wild :

" Another sighs for harmony and grace,

" And gentlest beauty.   Hence, when lightning flies

" The arch of heaven, and thunders rock the ground ;

" When furious whirlwinds rend the howling air,

" And ocean groaning from the lowest bed,

" Heaves his tempestuous billows to the sky,

" Amid the mighty uproar, while below,

" The nations tremble, Shakspeare looks abroad

" From some high cliff superior, and enjoys

" The elemental war."——   *Pleasures of Imag.*   Book iii.

The distinction due to Shakspeare in energy of poetry, to Michael Angelo in sculpture and painting, Handel may justly claim in the sister art; to him belongs the Majesty of Music. The merit of Handel is not confined: it is of that universal cast, that he may be styled the great musician of nature.   Though he was not able to pronounce the English with correctness, he thoroughly comprehended its nature and effects. In the funeral anthems, and the oratorios selected from the Scriptures, the words were principally chosen by himself; and the devotion of sounds, if the expression may be allowed, is in unison with the dignity, simple piety, and grandeur of the sacred writings. An English audience should estimate his abilities, by English compositions; and in beauty of expression and strong sense, he had there the greatest advantage: for what drama can be compared among all his Italian music, to the Acis and Galatea of Gay, L'Allegro and Penseroso of Milton, Dryden's unrivalled Ode to St. Cecilia, and Handel's great master-piece, the Messiah?

Words are, in relation to music, too frequently neglected, and considered as the mere vehicle for sounds; but sounds should be analogous to thoughts.

" To make the soul mount on a jig to heaven,"

is as absurd as to compose anthem music to ludicrous language. When sound and sense are judiciously united, in a fortunate illustration of each other; then articulation, the first principle in music, like light thrown upon a picture, discovers all the beauty of the subject, as well as merit of the execution.

The prejudice of fashion, and paucity of soprano voices in our own country, has too often occasioned an inadequate performance of Handel's music. Miss Linley proved to Handel, what Garrick was to Shakspeare; and those who recollect her captivating voice, feel the full merit of the great master's mind. A new light was thrown upon his compositions, and those who attended the Commemoration in Westminster Abbey, that spring-tide of harmony, have heard him in all his glory.

To specify Handel's claims to professional pre-eminence, would be a voluminous task; it would be no less than to select a variety of passages from each of his works, vocal as well as instrumental. Few men composed more; no man better. Handel was in music all things to all persons; considered generally he was irresistible, and master of the passions; the audience feel it, and in the language of that poetry, which he himself so happily made the strong example of his art,

" The list'ning crowd admire the lofty sound."

F

Such is the force and effect of his productions;—but he has the highest claim for moral and religious excellence. His pen was never debased to the disgraceful practice of an effeminate or seductive style of composition: it is entitled to the first attribute of praise.—It is sublime, affecting, animated, and devoted, without the gloom of superstition, to the service of God.

ANECDOTES

OF

JOHN CHRISTOPHER SMITH.

JOHN CHRISTOPHER SMITH.

From an Original Picture Painted by Zoffani.

Published May 1.1799. by Cadell & Davies Strand

ANECDOTES

OF

JOHN CHRISTOPHER SMITH.

JOHN CHRISTOPHER SMITH was born in 1712. His father John Christopher Schmidt, * of Anspach in Franconia, after receiving a good education in the university of Halle, married a lady with a portion of seven thousand crowns, and settled in his native city. He carried on a considerable branch of traffic in the woollen trade, in which he might have acquired a large fortune, had he not been seduced by his passion for music; when Handel arrived at Anspach in 1716, he renewed an acquaintance which had commenced at Halle, and soon became so captivated with that great master's powers, that he left his wife and children in Germany, and accompanied Handel to England, where he regulated the expences of his public performance, and filled the office of treasurer with great exactness and fidelity. On the fourth year of his residence in England, he sent for his wife and family, which consisted of a son and two daughters

* Schmidt was the German name corresponding with the English appellation Smith.

Soon after his arrival, his son, the subject of these Anecdotes, was sent to Clare's Academy, in Soho Square. During this early period of his life, he too imbibed a fondness for music, and gave signs of a strong propensity to that science; and as his passion increased with his years, Handel offered to become his master. Accordingly, in the thirteenth year of his age, he was taken from the Academy, and placed under the tuition of Handel.

When Smith was about fourteen, chance threw him in the way of Dr. Samuel Clarke, author of the Sermons on the Attributes of God, and of other celebrated writings, who behaved to him with the kindness of a father. He one day said to him, " you follow a dangerous profession, which may lead you into late hours, and excesses of all kinds, that will injure your constitution, and corrupt your morals. Come to my house whenever you are at leisure, and play with my boy." Dr. Clarke's son was then about twelve years of age. Young Smith accepted this invitation with gratitude, and passed many happy hours at the Doctor's; who was often one of the party, and would ride upon a broomstick with him and his son.

That good man and excellent divine, not unfrequently instructed him in the rudiments of natural and revealed religion, in a manner adapted to his capacity. In his advanced age, Mr. Smith often dwelt on the recollection of Dr. Clarke's extreme condescension and good nature. He seldom mentioned, without strong emotions of gratitude, the great advantage which he derived from his exhortations and instructions, and was often heard to declare, that to him, under Providence, he was principally indebted for those principles of morality, and firm belief in Revelation, which never forsook him.

Under the tuition of Handel Smith made so considerable a proficiency in music, that in the eighteenth year of his age, he commenced teacher, and instantly obtained, through his master's recommendation, and his own merit, so much employment, as to enable him to maintain himself without assistance from his father.

He often mentioned with conscious pride, that he was never in debt but once, when he borrowed ten guineas of old Schudi, and that he was not easy till he had returned the sum. His prudence, however, never degenerated into narrow parsimony. He once met with a family in the greatest distress, and though he was at that time worth but one guinea, he gave half to them. A gentleman, whose daughter he taught, being informed of this humane action, gave him five guineas, as a mark of approbation. In this present, the poor family participated.

It was Smith's good fortune to become acquainted with Dr. Arbuthnot, who behaved to him with the affection of a father, and contributed, by his skill and advice, to the preservation of his life. At the age of eighteen he had so greatly injured his health, by intense application, that he was declared by Dr. Mead to be in a decline. Arbuthnot was of opinion, that relaxation and change of air might possibly restore him; and having an house at Highgate, invited him to pass the summer in that healthy situation. The Doctor told him that he would certainly fall a victim to his application, if he did not relax; and though he lent him an horse, would not suffer him to ride to

London, lest he might be tempted to resume his studies.. By this kind care, his health was so far re-established, that he was again enabled to follow his profession. Thus the Doctor verified Pope's eulogium.

" He knows his art, but not his trade."

At Dr. Arbuthnot's house he frequently met Swift, Pope, Gay, and Congreve; a society highly improving to a young man. He observed that they never seemed desirous of uttering wise sayings, or witty repartees, but the conversation usually turned upon interesting subjects, when their talents and knowledge were displayed without ostentation. Sensible that Pope had no taste for music, he took an opportunity of inquiring what motive could induce him to celebrate Handel's praise so highly in his Dunciad. Pope replied, that merit, in every branch or science, ought to be encouraged; that the extreme illiberality with which many persons had joined to ruin Handel, in opposing his Operas, called forth his indignation; and though nature had denied his being gratified by Handel's uncommon talents in the musical line, yet when his powers were generally acknowledged, he thought it incumbent upon him to pay a tribute due to genius.

Although Handel had instructed his pupil in the rudiments of music, yet he could not stoop to the drudgery of teaching composition; and the scholar finding that he had not acquired sufficient knowledge, applied to Dr. Pepusch* and Rosengrave,+ from both of whom, in

---

* John Christopher Pepusch, called by Sir John Hawkins one of the greatest theoretic musicians of the modern times, was born at Berlin in 1667, and acquired such an early reputation for his skill and execution, that he was appointed, at the age of fourteen,

particular from Roseingrave, he derived great advantage. With a view to profit by Roseingrave's kindness, he took lodgings in the same

to teach the Electoral Prince, afterwards Frederick William, the harpsichord. About the twentieth year of his age he went to Holland, and came to England after the Revolution, where he settled. Having attracted notice by various musical publications, he obtained the degree of Doctor of Music in the university of Oxford. He was employed by the Duke of Chandos, as his master of the chapel at Cannons, and composed many anthems, together with the morning and evening services. He set to music several masques and pieces for the Theatre; and assisted Gay in selecting the tunes for the Beggar's Opera. Having married Margaretta de l'Epine, a celebrated singer, who quitted the stage with a fortune of ten thousand pounds, he not long afterwards relinquished composition; applied himself chiefly to the theory of music; and was fond of explaining the mysteries of the science to young professors, which induced Mr. Smith to court his assistance.

In 1717, he was appointed organist of the Charter House, which afforded him an adequate retreat, well suited to his time of life, and love of study. Here he was visited and consulted as an oracle; not only by young musical students, to whom he was always kind and communicative, but even by masters.

At the latter period of his life, he devoted himself to the study of Grecian music, and endeavoured to illustrate the doctrine of Isaac Vossius, concerning the rythm of the ancients. He was elected a Fellow of the Royal Society in 1746, and died in 1752, aged eighty-five. He was buried in the chapel of the Charter House; and several members of the Academy of Ancient Music, of which he was one of the original founders, and principal supporters, gratefully erected a monument to his memory.

If it be true what is said of him, that he treated all music, in which there was any fancy or invention, with sovereign contempt, and that he did not acquiesce in Handel's superior merit, calling him a good practical musician; his kindness in instructing Smith, who was the scholar and adorer of Handel, in the theory of music, reflects great honour on his candour and liberality of sentiment.

† Thomas Roseingrave, the son of Daniel Roseingrave, first organist of the Cathedral

house, in Wigmore-street, Mary-le-Bone, and received great advantage from his instruction. During this time, Roseingrave was a constant guest at his table, which was the only recompence he would ever receive. Smith always mentioned his name in terms of gratitude, and related anecdotes of his kind and friendly instructor.

of Salisbury, and in 1698 of St. Patrick's, Dublin. He received a classical education, which he completed at the Irish university, and was intended for one of the learned professions; but though he was a very good scholar, his love for music led him to apply with so much zeal to that study, that his father, foreseeing that it would impede his success in any other line, permitted him to follow the bent of his genius, and sent him to Italy, where he became the friend of Scarlatti. On quitting Italy, he settled in London, and obtained the place of organist to St. George's church, Hanover Square. There were three candidates, Roseingrave, Stanley, who was then a very young man, and Topham, who, besides his knowledge in music, was an adept in the pugilistic art. Roseingrave played first upon the organ, and his performance charmed and astonished every person present, and no one more than Topham; who observed, he could never stand in competition with him for music, but humorously added, that he would box with him whenever he pleased. Roseingrave was elected.

His reputation was at this period so high, that on commencing teacher, he might have gained one thousand pounds a year; but an unfortunate event reduced him to extreme distress.

Among Roseingrave's scholars, was a young lady to whom he was greatly attached, and whose affections he had gained; but her father, who intended to give her a large fortune, did not approve of her marrying a musician, and forbade Roseingrave his house. This disappointment affected his brain, and he never entirely recovered the shock. He neglected his scholars, and lost his business. He lived upon fifty pounds per annum, which his place produced, and was often in indigence. He was perfectly rational upon every subject, but the one nearest his heart; whenever that was mentioned, he was quite insane. In the latter part of his life, he was invited by his brother to reside with him, in Ireland, where he remained till his death.

Under these preceptors Smith made so rapid a progress, that in the twentieth year of his age he composed *Teraminta*, an English opera. According to a date written in his own hand, it was finished the 11th of October, 1732, and performed in the same year. The words were written by Henry Carey.* His invention was so fertile, that in the beginning of the ensuing year, he set to music another opera called Ulysses, which was likewise peformed; the words by Humphreys.

At the age of twenty-four, Mr. Smith married the daughter of Mr. Packenham, a gentleman of good fortune, in Ireland. He had reason to suppose that she was entitled to a fortune of three thousand pounds; but he never received any portion. They lived together nearly six years, and they had several children; but none survived the age of two years. She died of a decline. Her brother was afterwards created Lord Longford.

About the age of thirty-four, he taught the grandson of old Peter Waters (whose worthless memory is recorded by Pope) : the young man appeared to form a friendship for Smith, and, succeeding to his grandfather's fortune, offered to settle on him an annuity of three hundred pounds, if he would relinquish teaching, and accompany him to the South of France, where he was going for the recovery of his health; being so great an invalid, that he was obliged to be lifted in and out of his carriage. Smith, after consulting his friends, accepted the proposal. The expectation of a good income for life, together with the

* Harry Carey composed the popular song of " God save great George our king." But although he had much genius for music, he was ignorant of the rules of composition, and applied to Smith to adapt a base to the air.

advantages which he must derive from going abroad with a sensible man, who lived in a genteel and pleasant society, induced him to throw himself on the generosity of a person, whom he conceived to be liberal, and whom he knew to be an agreeable companion. He continued with him abroad for two or three years.

It appears, from several dates annexed to his compositions, that during the three years of his residence abroad, he never intermitted his musical studies: he finished the last act of his opera of *Dario*, in 1746, and began to compose Metastasio's *Artaserse*, at Aix in Provence, in December, 1748. He passed some time at Geneva, where he formed an intimate acquaintance with some English gentlemen, distinguished for rank, learning, and talents. Among these must be particularly specified the celebrated Benjamin Stillingfleet; Mr. Price of Foxley, Herefordshire; Mr. Windham of Felbrig, in Norfolk; Mr. Aldworth Neville; Mr. Benjamin Tate of Mitcham, in Surrey; and the Rev. Dr. Dampier, afterwards Dean of Durham.

About this period Handel became blind. His surgeon, Mr. Sharp, having asked him if he was able to continue playing the organ in public, for the performance of the Oratorios? Handel replied in the negative. Sharp recommended Stanley, as a person whose memory never failed; upon which Handel burst into a loud laugh, and said, " Mr. Sharp, have you never read the Scriptures? do you not remember, if the blind lead the blind, they will both fall into the ditch?" In this dilemma, Handel sent for his pupil to assist him in the approaching Lent season. Smith could not decline Handel's invitation; and Mr. Waters resolved to return to England, as well to enjoy his friend's company, as because his sister, who was one of the party, was in a lingering and dangerous illness.

When Smith played the organ at the Theatre, during the first year of Handel's blindness, Samson was performed, and Beard sung, with great feeling,

" Total eclipse—no sun, no moon,
" All dark amid the blaze of noon."—

The recollection that Handel had set this air to music, with the view of the blind composer then sitting by the organ, affected the audience so forcibly, that many persons present were moved even to tears.

A year after Smith's return to England, Mrs. Waters died. A short time before her death, she advised him not to be deceived by the apparent kindness of her brother, who she knew had not named him in his will, and she much feared that he never intended .to perform his promise. At her death, she left Mr. Smith five hundred pounds. In the ensuing summer, Mr. Waters proposed going to Spa, and invited Smith to accompany him, who, recollecting the intimation of Mrs. Waters, expressed apprehensions that he would not perform his promise, as he had not given him any security; upon which Waters said, angrily, " I have left you in my will the annuity I promised; won't you take my word?"—" No," replied Smith, " I would not give a pinch of snuff for your word." And, in fact, he was in the right; for Mr. Waters died within a few months, without naming Smith in his will, which had been made eight years. On this disappointment he resumed his occupation, and soon raised himself into high estimation.

At this period, Smith derived great pleasure, as well as advantage, from the friendships he had formed at Geneva. He always dwelt with extreme satisfaction on the many happy hours he had passed at Mitcham with Mr. Tate, and at Foxley with Mr. Price; from which places he dates many of his compositions. Mr. Price, whom Smith mentions as an excellent composer, encouraged him in his labours, and wrote the poetry for the Oratorio of *Judith*. At the house of Mr. Price, who had married Lord Barrington's sister, Smith became acquainted with that family; from all of whom, and particularly from Mr. Daines Barrington, he received many marks of friendship.

About this time he formed a close intimacy with Garrick, whom he often met at the house of his friend, Mr. Venables, a wine merchant, in Covent-Garden. Smith was highly delighted with the captivating manners and convivial talents of that inimitable actor; and Garrick was no less pleased with his frank and unassuming manner. Their friendship was afterwards heightened by mutual interest.

In 1754, Smith successfully displayed his talents for composition, in the Fairies, a musical drama, altered from the Midsummer-Night's Dream of Shakspeare; it was performed at the Theatre Royal Drury-lane, under the auspices of Garrick. The day before the first representation, Garrick informed Smith, that he was afraid there was a strong party to condemn the piece, because Lord Middlesex (afterwards Duke of Dorset) had taken forty places in the boxes, and so formidable a number must have some bad design. Smith replied, he could not be induced to believe Lord Middlesex had any intention to injure him, for he had never disobliged his lordship, who had always been remarkably kind to him. When the piece was performed, it proved true indeed, that Lord Middlesex had engaged so large a part of the house, but with a kind intention of supporting the piece, which had a long and continued success. The words of Shakspeare's Mid-summer-Night's Dream, are light and airy, the music is well adapted to the words, and the children who performed the fairy part, were so admirably suited to the several characters, particularly Miss Young, who represented the fairy queen, that the performance was reckoned a chef-d'œuvre.

The great success of the Fairies, encouraged Smith to make another attempt in the same species of composition, by setting to music the songs in the Tempest. But although the airs were by no means in-ferior to those in the Fairies, yet the piece did not meet with the success it deserved; a principal cause of this failure, was probably owing to the negligent manner in which it was brought on the stage. The season was too far advanced, and the decorations were in-different.

Smith having remonstrated against this method of proceeding, Garrick alleged that his principal actors threatened to leave him, if these musical pieces, in which they had no concern, were so frequently performed on the stage. This behaviour occasioned a breach; and their estrangement continued until Mr. Clutterbuck, a friend of both parties, persuaded Smith to forget and forgive. The two friends met at his house, and the intimacy was renewed. Thus Garrick realized that part of his character, given by Goldsmith in his excellent poem of Retaliation:—

" He cast off his friends as a huntsman his pack,

" For he knew, when he pleas'd he could whistle them back."

It must not be omitted, that when the Tempest, set to music by Purcell, was represented at the Concert of Ancient Music, the celebrated air, " Full fathom five," by Smith, was substituted for that of the original composer. It was universally admired, and has ever since been retained. This air has been harmonized as a glee by Corfe, organist of the King's chapel, with the greatest effect.

Handel continued to employ Smith senior as his treasurer, and their friendly intercourse was uninterrupted, till they both went to Tunbridge, about four years before Handel's death. But as long friendships are sometimes dissolved by the most trivial circumstances, they quarrelled there, and Smith senior left Handel in an abrupt manner, which so enraged him, that he declared he would never see him again; and though friends interfered to promote a reconciliation, their interference was for a long time without effect. After this quarrel, Handel took Smith one day by the hand, and said he was determined to put his name in the place of his father, in his will: Smith declared, if he persisted in that resolution, he would instantly quit him, and never more assist in the Oratorios; " for," added he, " what will the world think, if you set aside my father, and leave his legacy to me? they will suppose I tried, and succeeded in undermining him for my own advantage." Handel yielded to these just remonstrances.

About three weeks before Handel's death, he desired Smith junior to receive the sacrament with him. Smith asked him how he could communicate, when he was not at peace with all the world, and especially when he was at enmity with his former friend; who, though he might have offended him once, had been faithful and affectionate to him for thirty years. Handel was so much affected by this representation, that he was immediately reconciled; and dying soon after (in the year 1759), left Smith senior two thousand four hundred pounds, having before given him one thousand pounds. To Mr. Smith he left all his manuscript music* in score, his harpsichord, on which almost all that music had been composed, his portrait painted by Denner, and his bust by Roubillac.

It had been Handel's wish, that all the manuscript music should be assigned to Oxford, and preserved in the university library; and with that attention to his posthumous fame, and regard to an university which had been sensible of his merits, he proposed to give Smith a legacy of three thousand pounds, if he would resign his claim to the promise which Handel had made to him. But he had too much enthusiasm for the art, and too great a veneration for the production of so able a composer, his friend and instructor, to relinquish, for any pecuniary consideration, so inestimable a prize; and Handel faithfully fulfilled his promise at his death. Many of Handel's compositions were afterwards pirated from scores lent by Smith, and from others which had not been returned by performers. Too inattentive to his own advantage, he never prosecuted the printers, and many editions were published.

---

* The Great Frederick, King of Prussia, offered Smith two thousand pounds for Handel's manuscripts; but he was unwilling to let such a treasure go out of England.

H

Smith, after Handel's death, carried on the Oratorios in partner-
ship with Mr. Stanley,* whose professional abilities, and estimable

* John Stanley was born in 1713. His father had a lucrative employment in the
Post-office. In his second year he became blind by the following circumstance :—he
fell down with a china bason in his hand ; the bason breaking, a pointed fragment cut
through one of his eyes, which occasioned the loss of the other.

Having attained the age of seven, he began to learn music ; not because he had discovered the smallest propensity to it, or because his father was musical himself, or fond
of the art : he was advised to have his son instructed on the harpsichord as an amuse-
ment, to which he consented ; but without any hopes that it would be advantageous to
his progress in life. His first master was Reading, a scholar of Blow, and organist of
Hackney. He continued under Reading only a few months ; during which time, the
difficulty of receiving information was so great, that he made scarcely any progress.
The boy, however, discovering great pleasure in the occupation, his father placed him
with Dr. Green, organist of St. Paul's.

Under this scientific master Stanley made a most rapid progress, and attained so great
a proficiency, that when eleven, he was chosen organist of the church of Allhallows,
Bread-street ; at fourteen, he was appointed organist of St. Andrew's, Holborn, in preference to a great number of candidates ; at sixteen, he was elected by the Honourable
Society of the Middle Temple, one of their organists. These two places he retained
to his death. His abilities as a master acquired him a handsome income. He had great
facility in teaching ; and from his patience in instructing, and his address, was always
much beloved by his pupils.

" Few persons," observes Dr. Burney, " have passed a more active life in every
branch of his art, than this extraordinary musician ; having been not only a neat, pleas-
ing, and accurate performer, but a natural and agreeable composer, and an intelligent
instructor. He continued to teach until 1760 ; when, on the death of Handel, he en-
tered into an engagement with Smith, to carry on the Oratorios for fourteen years. At
the end of that time, Smith retiring from the musical world, Stanley engaged with Mr.

character, rendered him a very desirable associate. On the decease of his father, Smith declined receiving any share of the small fortune, which was left among his three children, and divided it between his two sisters.

It was Mr. Smith's peculiar turn of disposition, not to live much with the professors of music, Pepusch, Roseingrave, and Handel excepted; and the friendships he formed in life were with men of a different profession, or persons of fortune, character, and abilities.

Linley for the same purpose, and was honoured with the patronage of their Majesties. In 1785, his health being much impaired, he retired from business. He died the 19th of May, 1786."

He was a most cheerful and lively companion, of a placid and serene temper, and perfectly contented with his situation. He was often heard to say, that he would not receive his sight, if it was in his power. He felt himself, he said, perfectly happy under his present circumstances; and should have so much to learn and unlearn, that all would be uncertainty and confusion.

The loss of his sight was amply repaid by the acuteness of his hearing, and the extreme sensibility of his touch. He could find his way even through the narrowest passages and alleys of London; he could ascertain the size of an apartment by the sound of his voice; he recollected the voices of those whom he had not seen for many years; and he played at whist with a facility that astonished all who saw him. The cards were marked with a needle at one corner; but the marks were so small as to be almost imperceptible; yet he was never embarrassed, and required only that the card which was played should be mentioned. He was fond of riding, and an excellent judge of horses: he discovered the proportions by feeling, and judged of its paces by the ear; and he once prevented a friend from purchasing a horse that was lame. He married Miss Harland, daughter of Captain Harland, in the East India service, by whom he had no issue.

Among those with whom he was closely connected, was Dr. Coxe,*
Physician Extraordinary to the King; who was highly noticed for his
professional abilities, and much beloved and esteemed for his amiable
virtues and private character. The friendship which the Doctor enter-
tained for Mr. Smith, and the high opinion which he formed of his
integrity, was so great, that on his death bed, he recommended his
wife to consult Mr. Smith on every emergency.

Desirous of proving his good wishes for the welfare of her family,
anxious to render every assistance in his power, and convinced that
his principles of good will could not be carried into effect, without a
closer alliance than that of friendship, at a proper season he proposed
himself to her in marriage, that he might be at once, and effectually,
a father to her children. Her consent was succeeded by the most
unequivocal demonstrations of the generosity and candour of his
declarations. His kindness to all her children, invariably, in sickness
and in health, his anxiety for their welfare, his wish to further their
interest, his readiness to promote it, his satisfaction at every little advantage that accrued to them, were convincing indications of a kind
and affectionate heart.

Soon after the accession of his present Majesty, Mr. Smith was
introduced to the Royal Family. His introduction was principally
occasioned by the following circumstance: Pinchbeck being employed
by the Earl of Bute to construct a barrel organ of extraordinary

---

* Dr. Coxe was distinguished by Mr. Melmoth's elegant pen, in his Fitzosborne's
Letters, under the name of Philotes; and his wife, who afterwards espoused Mr. Smith,
was mentioned under the appellation of Aspasia.

size, requested Smith to superintend the work; which he at first declined, but, on application from his Lordship, afterwards complied. Langshaw, a very ingenious artist, was employed; and, under Smith's directions, set the barrels with so much delicacy and taste, as to convey a warm idea of the impression which the hand gives on the instrument. The organ* was esteemed a masterpiece in musical mechanism; and Lord Bute was so well pleased with his success, that he was desirous of making an adequate compensation for the trouble. Smith declined all pecuniary gratification; and hinted, that he should think his pains more than amply repaid, if, through his Lordship's recommendation, the King would condescend to patronize the Oratorios. Lord Bute accordingly represented Mr. Smith in so favourable a light, that the King honoured the Oratorios with his presence; at first, six nights out of eleven; afterwards, for several years, he went the whole eleven, which was a great support, and brought much company to the house, although the Oratorios had then ceased to be the favourite entertainment of the public; his Majesty almost *stood single* in his approbation of the great Handel, when the preference for Italian music was becoming universal.

The Princess Dowager of Wales having expressed an inclination to engage some person of eminence in the musical profession, to attend twice a week, and give her instruction on the harpsichord, Lord Bute said, that he would recommend a master, who he was sure would be acceptable; but before he could name him, her Royal Highness inter-

---

* The size of the barrels was considerably larger than any that had been made. The organ itself was also much larger than had ever been used for barrels. After the death of the Earl of Bute, this organ was purchased by the Earl of Shaftesbury.

rupting him, said, she had already fixed on a person; and immediately mentioned Mr. Smith. He was accordingly placed in the
Princess's household, and attended at Carlton House once or twice a
week, with a salary of two hundred pounds.

The Princess was uncommonly gracious and condescending, and
derived so much satisfaction and improvement from his instructions,
that she was often heard to say, that in her advanced age, she had
acquired a new taste for music, and had received notions of harmony,
which she had never before experienced. She was fond of his musical
compositions, and several of them, particularly the Oratorio of Gideon,
were performed at Carlton House.

In 1772 he lost his great benefactress, and was deeply affected. To
relieve his mind he undertook a task, suitable to the melancholy occasion. He set the funeral service to music, which he had long medi-
tated; and his mind was so occupied, that during several nights he
enjoyed no rest. It is composed with great pathos and expression.

After the death of the Princess Dowager, the King graciously continued to Mr. Smith the same pension out of his privy purse, free of all deductions, which greatly contributed to the ease and comfort of his life.

In a mind so constituted as that of Mr. Smith, where liberality and
disinterestedness were distinguishing features, it is easy to be supposed
that gratitude would be no less conspicuous; and that the conduct of
the King, in graciously patronizing the Oratorios, his condescension
to him, whenever he was honoured with an audience, and his conti-

nuing to him the pension of' two hundred pounds, paid by the Princess Dowager of Wales, and drawn from the privy purse (free from all customary deductions), and that pension graciously presented to him from his Majesty's own hand, would naturally operate on a disposition peculiarly sensible. He accordingly expressed that gratitude in a way which he thought most acceptable to his Sovereign; and in the fulness of his heartfelt acknowledgment, presented to the King the rich legacy which Handel had left him, of all his manuscript music, in score. The harpsichord, so remarkable for the ivory being indented by Handel's continued exertions, and on which, as has been already related, the far greater part of his music had been composed; and his bust, by Roubillac, he sent afterwards to Windsor Castle. Of all that his great instructor had bequeathed him, he only reserved to himself the portrait painted by Denner.

The produce from the Oratorios answered Mr. Smith's expectations every year, and in 1769, when Miss Linley sung, the advantage was increased in a great degree. But when she declined singing in public, and the King was prevented from appearing in public, by the Queen's lying-in during Lent, the Oratorios were much deserted, and performed almost to empty houses. Smith therefore, thought it most advisable to resign the conduct of these performances, lest, by persisting, he should have the misfortune to lose what he had formerly gained. He quitted the neighbourhood of London, and retired to a house he had recently bought, in Brock-street, Bath.

In 1785, Mrs. Smith died. Mr. Smith, who had ever been tenderly attached to her, was most severely afflicted at her loss. Grief so shook his frame that he appeared visibly declining, but the strength of his constitution enabled him to recover this blow. He lived beloved and respected from his benevolence, which led him on all occasions to assist the distressed, as far as his moderate fortune permitted; and he frequently denied himself gratifications and indulgences, that by these little sacrifices he might be able to relieve the necessitous. His benevolence made him take pleasure in improving young people; and at the advanced age of eighty-one, he instructed a few young ladies who had genius for music.

Several persons of high rank and merit, who had formerly known him, usually called upon him when they came to Bath, and expressed their regard for him, as a man equally respectable for genius and integrity. He used to observe upon these occasions,—" I am in general dead to the vanities of the world, but I own myself flattered by these marks of attention: there was a time when I was courted, because I could amuse and entertain; but now the attention that is shewn me, when I can give no entertainment, can only arise from the esteem that the world pays to my character."

In September, 1795, Smith was seized with a disorder, which terminated his existence in eight days. At first he suffered great pain, but being relieved by opiates, remained in a state of composure. From the first moment of his illness, to the instant of his death, he displayed the brightest example of a true Christian and a benevolent mind. He expired on the third of October, in the eighty-fifth year of his age.

Smith's last effort of composition was the Redemption, an Oratorio compiled from the Scriptures, by the Reverend William Coxe. It was intended for public performance, but the difficulty of procuring proper voices frustrated the plan.

Although a great enthusiast in his profession, yet after his retirement, he seldom amused himself at the harpsichord. He did not, however, desist from his usual application either from satiety, disgust, or want of feeling, but rather from extreme sensibility. His style of playing was singularly animated and impressive, and his mind was totally absorbed in his occupation. But when age had produced such a tremor of the hands, as prevented him from executing light and delicate passages, he felt so much mortification on finding his inability to touch the instrument in his accustomed manner, and to produce an effect corresponding with his exquisite feelings, that he thought it prudent to relinquish his favourite employment.

When the Commemoration of Handel was celebrated with such wonderful effect in Westminster Abbey, under the direction of Joah Bates, Esq. the King was desirous that Smith should be present at the performance, and sent him a gracious and pressing invitation to come to London for that purpose. His Majesty assured him hat he should be admitted without difficulty into a commodious seat in the Abbey, and that he should receive every accommodation during his residence in town. Smith was fully sensible of this gracious mark of condescension; but declined the honour with reluctance, apprehensive that from his advanced age, so exquisitely powerful a performance of the works of his great master, would excite such emotions as might too much affect his feeble frame.

As a professional man, he was unobtrusive. His talents were no less solid than brilliant; equally adapted to the fanciful and elegant style of composition, exemplified in the opera of the Fairies, and to the serious cast of sacred music, displayed in his Oratorios and Funeral Anthem.

With a quiet but not inactive turn of mind, he did not pursue the exertion of his faculties unremittingly to his own profit. From constitution he was of a tranquil disposition, little calculated to struggle against the intrigues which modest merit must encounter in a science in which the professors, as well as performers, too often appear peculiarly irritable, and,

——————— " too fond to rule alone,
" Bear, like the Turk, no brother near the throne."

Though he loved the art, he found himself unequal to the trade, and had not courage to encounter obstacles, or patience to reconcile contending interests.

His spirit was so liberal and independent, that he could never bend to the circumstances of the times, nor sufficiently consult the taste of the age, if he deemed that taste frivolous or capricious : he could not be induced to sacrifice his own feelings and judgment to expected profit.

His Operas of the Fairies and the Tempest, Lessons for the Harpsichord, and the Oratorio of Paradise Lost, are the chief productions with which the world is acquainted. A list of his works is given in the Appendix

But if his own compositions did not sufficiently speak for him, his highest commendation would be the praise of Handel. To have been called upon by that great musician to supply his place at the organ, testifies his abilities as a performer, and conductor of a band.

His genius was by no means confined to music; he was fond of reading, had a taste for all the liberal arts, and formed a small but interesting collection of pictures.

In stature, Mr. Smith was below the middle size; he was upright in his walk, polite in his address; had hands delicately formed, blue and impressive eyes, and his whole countenance remarkably open. Though naturally grave, he was alive to cheerful conversation. His laugh was peculiarly unrestrained; not loud and boisterous, but indicating that heartfelt satisfaction which surrenders the understanding, without folly, to the cheerful and social impulse of the moment.

In his private character, he united many estimable and agreeable qualities; he was sincere, benevolent, and humane; scrupulously just in all moral obligations, and had a devout sense of religion, untinctured by superstition. In society he was cheerful, and his conversation was enlivened with pleasant sallies and quick repartee. In domestic life he was benevolent and affectionate; and was kind, almost to a fault, to his domestics. The same principle remained with him in the hour of sickness and of death; as he was anxious in his last moments to spare his attendants all unnecessary trouble.

He was particularly careful to impress on the minds of his adopted children, a full conviction that Christianity is alone sufficient to happiness; and that a disbelief of divine revelation would insensibly lead to every species of vice and misery. A letter which he wrote twenty years before his death to one of his adopted sons, when at the university, fully proves that this principle was not dictated by sickness or old age, but was the genuine result of firm conviction and settled belief.

" My dear Friend,

" I am much obliged to you for your affectionate letter, as it con firmed me in the opinion I always had, of the goodness and rectitude of your heart, which I hope you will always preserve; and which, give me leave to say, is no very easy task in so degenerate an age as that we live in at present. Much of your future happiness will, in a great measure, depend on the choice you make of friends; you must be particularly careful in so nice a point; for it is not sufficient his being barely a good moral man, that will qualify him for your friendship, there is still something more required, and that is, he ought to be a Christian; and unless he has really those principles in him, you cannot safely take him to your bosom: for although he would not wrong you of a farthing, yet he will not scruple (if he be an Atheist or Deist) to endeavour with great pains to imbibe into you principles, that will not only make you very unhappy in this life, but, what is worse, hazard your eternal salvation in the next.

" My dear friend, I have only cautioned you against one set of men, and to me the most dangerous; others may lead you into many indiscretions, but not so fatal in their consequences. All that I have farther to say at present is, that I hope on all occasions you will look on me as your sincere friend, and not hide any part of your conduct from me; and in return for such a confidence reposed, I will promise you, that it will be the pleasure and study of my life to make yours as happy as I possibly can.

I am, my dear friend,

Most affectionately yours,

J. C. Smith."

In the last years of his life he was particularly careful to soften his manners, to correct his temper, and to render himself as faultless as possible. He verified that maxim of his favourite Madame de Sevigné, " Quand on n'est plus jeune, c'est alors qu'il faut se perfectionner, et tâcher de regagner, par les bonnes qualités, ce qu'on perd du côté des agréables."

His life was extended beyond the common period of human existence, without deviating from the paths of integrity and honour. The testimony of several who were his contemporaries in the early season of his days, and of many who were witnesses, at a later period,

" To the noiseless tenour of his way,"

who saw and conversed with him daily, who are still living, and can appreciate his merits, may be adduced as a proof of this assertion.

APPENDIX.

LIST

OF

MR. SMITH'S COMPOSITIONS,

IN THE POSSESSION OF HIS DAUGHTER-IN-LAW, LADY RIVERS.

ENGLISH OPERAS.

Teraminta, an Opera. Three Acts. *Composed by J. C. Smith, Oct.* 11, 1732. Performed the same year. The words by Henry Carey.

Ulysses, an Opera. *Composed by J. C. Smith, April* 11, 1733. Performed the same year. The words by Mr. Humphreys.

The Fairies; or Midsummer-Night's Dream, an Opera. Three Acts. Published, 1756. The words principally taken from Shakspeare, said to be by Garrick.

The Tempest. Three Acts. Published, 1756. From Shakspeare. The words said to be by Garrick.

Medea; only two Acts finished. The words by Mr. Stillingfleet.

ITALIAN OPERAS.

Dario. *Fine de l'Atto primo, London, March* 8, 1746. *Fine de l'Atto secondo, London, June* 6, 1746. *Fine de l'Atto terzo, Rotterdam, Sept.* 5, 1746.

Issipile. 1746.

Il Ciro Riconosciuto. Three Acts. Words by Metastasio. No date or signature.

ORATORIOS.

Paradise Lost. Three Parts. Words by Stillingfleet. *Mitcham, December* 1, 1757. *Finished at Foxley, July* 29, 1758. Dr. Burney says it was performed in 1760.

David's Lamentation over Saul and Jonathan. *Composed by J. C. Smith, March* 20, 1738. Burney says it was performed in 1748.

ORATORIOS.

Nabal. Words by Dr. Morell. Performed in 1764. Compiled partly from Handel.

Gideon. 1769. Words by Dr. Morell. Compiled partly from Handel.

Judith, in Three Acts. Words by the late Mr. Price. Thus noted by Mr. Smith: *By Robert Price, Esq. of Foxley, in Herefordshire: who was himself an excellent composer in music.*

Jehosaphat. Two Acts. I can find no trace that this Oratorio was ever performed.

Redemption. Three Acts. Never performed. Words from the Scripture, by the Rev. W. Coxe.

MISCELLANEOUS.

The Burial Service.

Winter: or Daphne. Pope's Pastoral on the death of Mrs. Tempest. *Jan.* 26, 1746.

The Seasons. Two Parts.

Fugues, 1754, 1756. Never published.

Lessons for the Harpsichord, published.

Thamesi, Isi, e Proteo. In honour of Frederick Prince of Wales.

FRAGMENTS.

A few scenes of Artaserse, by Metastasio. Dated in Mr. Smith's hand writing, *Aix en Provence,* 1749.

A Hunting Scene and Song, composed for Queen Caroline's Hermitage; but without date or note.

DUETT from the ORATORIO
of
David's Lamentation over Saul and Jonathan.

pride, On yon high Moun _ _ _ _ _ _ _ _ _ tain bleed _ _ _

pride,   On yon high Moun _ _ _ tain bleed _ _ _

_ _ _ _ _ ing lies   On yon high Mountain bleeding lies _ _ _

_ _ _ _ _ ing lies   On yon high Mountain bleeding lies _ _ _

thy Beau _ _ _ _ _

thy Beau _ _ _ _ _

_ _ _ ty's Pri _ _ _ _ _ _ _ de   on yon high

_ _ _ ty's Pri _ _ _ _ _ _ _ de on yon high moun _ _ _ _

moun - - - - tain - bleeding lies - - - - -

- - - - - - - - - tain bleeding lies - - - -

on yon high mountain bleeding lies

- - - - - - on yon high mountain bleeding lies

How

How have the mighty warriors

have the mighty warriors died

died   no   weeping   friend to   close their   eyes

no   weeping   friend to   close their   eyes How

How   have the mighty warriors   died   How

have the mighty warriors   died   How   have the mighty warriors

Song from the Opera of
MEDEA

She who lays that charm a _ side falls a

Victim to her pride

to her pride   fhe who lays that charm a__side   falls a

Vic__tim to her pride.

Recitative and Air from the Oratorio of
JUDITH

Oh rash presumtuous man; how hast thou dar'd to bind the Counsels of the Lord; unskill'd to fathom the weak fhallow heart of man; how canst thou fearchout God; and Comprehend his vast de_signs; for not within the bounds of these five days alone, but ev'ry day he may defend us.

With Resignation, let us wait the hour when

owes its birth

With Re_fig__nation let us wait   with Re_fig__nation let us

wait when sorrow shall be turnd be turnd to mirth be turnd to mirth

Nor vainly think nor vainly think to circum _ scribe that powr to which Cre _

_ation owes its birth with Resignation let us wait the hour nor vainly think to

cir_ _cumscribe that pow'r to which Cre_ation owes its birth to

which Cre _ a _ tion owes its birth.

24

Shall human Reason dare to scan and limit Pow'r di_

_vine   And shall that help__less Crea__ture Man   Om_

_ni_potence con__fine   Om__ni_potence con__fine   With.

Da Capo al Segno.

AIR

Impero al gus-to al Prode L'llomfol gode la Li _ ber_ta L'llomfol gode la

liber _ ta Lll fol go _ _ _ _ de liber _ ta

la liber_ta la liber_ta _ _ _ _

Alle Leggi sta som messo ch egli

stessoallor si fa - - - - - ch egli stesso allor

si fa ch egli stessoallor si fa

Dando im

Da Capo al Segno 𝄋

30

My hope is in thee Lord thou art swift to comfort

and wilt have mercy up—on thy afflicted Preserve me

Lord for in thee have I put my Trust.

Hautboi

SOLO

Andantino

Violini

Andantino

Thou art my

Shepherd thou wilt feed me wilt feed me in a green Pas_ _ _ _ture

solo

And bring me

forth be_fide the waters of Comfort and bring me forth be_fide the

For EU product safety concerns, contact us at Calle de José Abascal, 56–1°, 28003 Madrid, Spain or eugpsr@cambridge.org.

www.ingramcontent.com/pod-product-compliance
Ingram Content Group UK Ltd.
Pitfield, Milton Keynes, MK11 3LW, UK
UKHW051009240426
470322UK00018B/587